Let's Visit
THE UNITED STATES
A Passport Sticker Book

by David Gantz

FEATURING
A Removable Souvenir Passport And 70 Full-color Stickers
★ Turn to Back of Book ★

Little Simon

Simon & Schuster Building
Rockefeller Center
1230 Avenue of the Americas
New York, New York 10020

Copyright © 1989 by David Gantz

10 9 8 7 6 5 4 3 2

ISBN 0-671-67212-6

Frannie and Joey's jet plane circled New York City before landing at LaGuardia Airport.

"Look, Frannie," said Joey, "there are the United Nations buildings along the East River."

"And there's the Empire State Building and the Chrysler Building," replied Frannie.

That afternoon Frannie and Joey walked across the famous Brooklyn Bridge and looked at the skyline from the borough of Brooklyn.

The Statue of Liberty

The Brooklyn Bridge

The next day they took a helicopter tour of New York City. They flew over the Statue of Liberty on Liberty Island in New York Harbor.

In the state of Pennsylvania, Frannie and Joey visited the Pennsylvania Dutch country. They rode through the rich farmland in an old-fashioned horse and buggy.

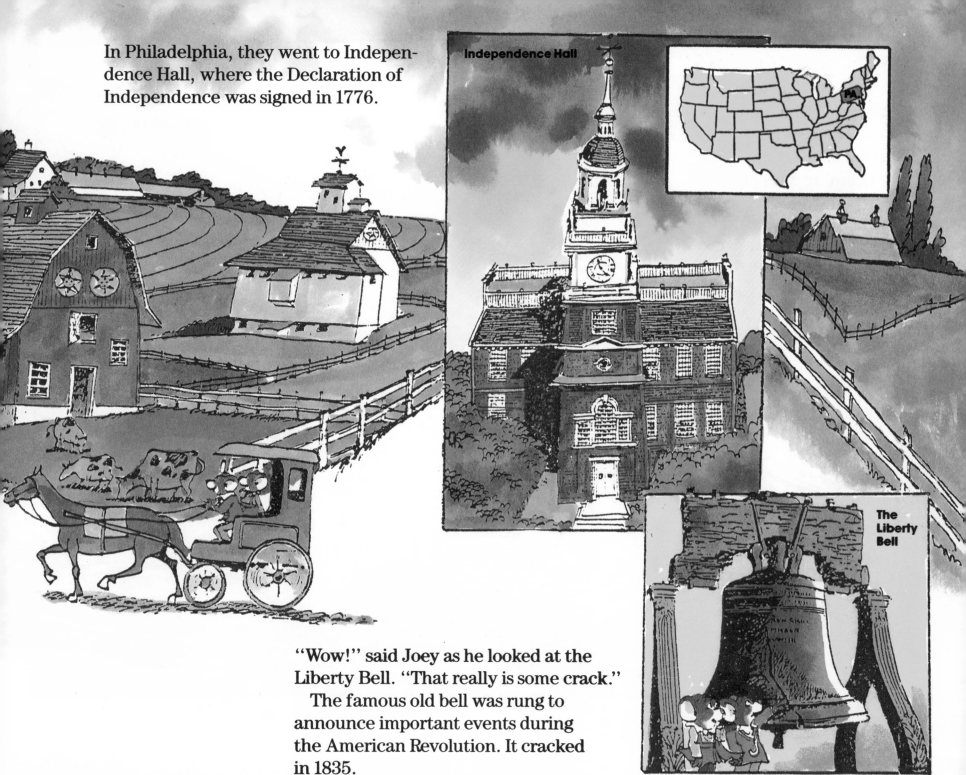

In Philadelphia, they went to Independence Hall, where the Declaration of Independence was signed in 1776.

Independence Hall

The Liberty Bell

"Wow!" said Joey as he looked at the Liberty Bell. "That really is some crack."
The famous old bell was rung to announce important events during the American Revolution. It cracked in 1835.

Frannie and Joey boarded an Amtrak train in Philadelphia and continued on to Washington, D.C. When they stood before the Capitol, they were beaming with pride.

"The Capitol is the place where the Senate and the House of Representatives meet," said Frannie.

The next afternoon they jogged past the White House, where the President lives and works. Both the Capitol and the White House were burned by British troops in 1814.

The Lincoln Memorial

D.C.

Later that afternoon Frannie and Joey visited the Lincoln Memorial.

Early on a summer morning, Frannie and Joey looked out on the harbor in Eastport, Maine.

"It's the first place in the United States to see the sun come up every day," Frannie explained.

A lobsterman told Joey, "Three-quarters of all the lobsters caught in America come from here."

"I'm going to eat a whole one all by myself for supper," said Joey.

A few days later they sailed down the Atlantic coast to Provincetown on the tip of Cape Cod, Massachusetts.

"Twenty-five miles away, on the other side of Cape Cod Bay," Joey said, "is Plymouth Rock, where the pilgrims landed."

Provincetown

The Old North Church, Boston

Frannie and Joey then went on to Boston where they saw some historical sights, including the Old North Church.

"The British are coming! The British are coming!" shouted Joey, remembering how Paul Revere began his famous ride.

Frannie and Joey left New England for a trip through the southern states. It was like a trip through American history.

In Georgia, they stopped at Stone Mountain to see the great granite carvings of Jefferson Davis, Robert E. Lee, and Stonewall Jackson, who led the Confederate army in the Civil War.

In Virginia they visited Williamsburg and saw what life was like before the American Revolution. They went to a blacksmith's shop, ate peanut soup and cornmeal cakes, and marched along with a fife and drum corps.

Miami Beach

Williamsburg

"This looks like a city from the future!" said Joey, gazing from the airplane window at the skyline of Miami Beach, Florida.

"It's the largest beach resort in the whole world," Frannie added as their plane headed northwest toward St. Louis and the Mississippi River.

Frannie and Joey looked out from the upper deck of the *Natchez* as the great sternwheeler kicked up a watery foam in the Mississippi River.

"The *Natchez* used to race other sternwheelers between St. Louis and New Orleans," said Frannie.

As they left St. Louis, they saw the 630-foot-high Gateway Arch and thought about the pioneers and their wagon trains that headed west from the city.

Gateway Arch, St. Louis

On their way south down the big river, Frannie and Joey stopped to visit the Melrose House in Natchez, Mississippi, an old southern mansion.

The Melrose House

On the outskirts of New Orleans, they paddled a flat-bottomed boat through the Louisiana bayou swamps.

"This sure is a spooky looking place," said Joey.

"Pirates used to hide out here," replied Frannie.

A Bayou Swamp

Before heading west, Frannie and Joey flew to Niagara, on the border between New York State and Canada.

"Wow! It's huge!" said Frannie when she and Joey first saw the great falls.

"We should have brought an umbrella," Joey laughed. Even standing at the top of the falls they could feel the white spray from the mountains of water cascading down, down, down....

There are two sets of falls at Niagara: the 173-foot-high Horseshoe Falls, on the Canadian side, and the 182-foot-high American Falls.

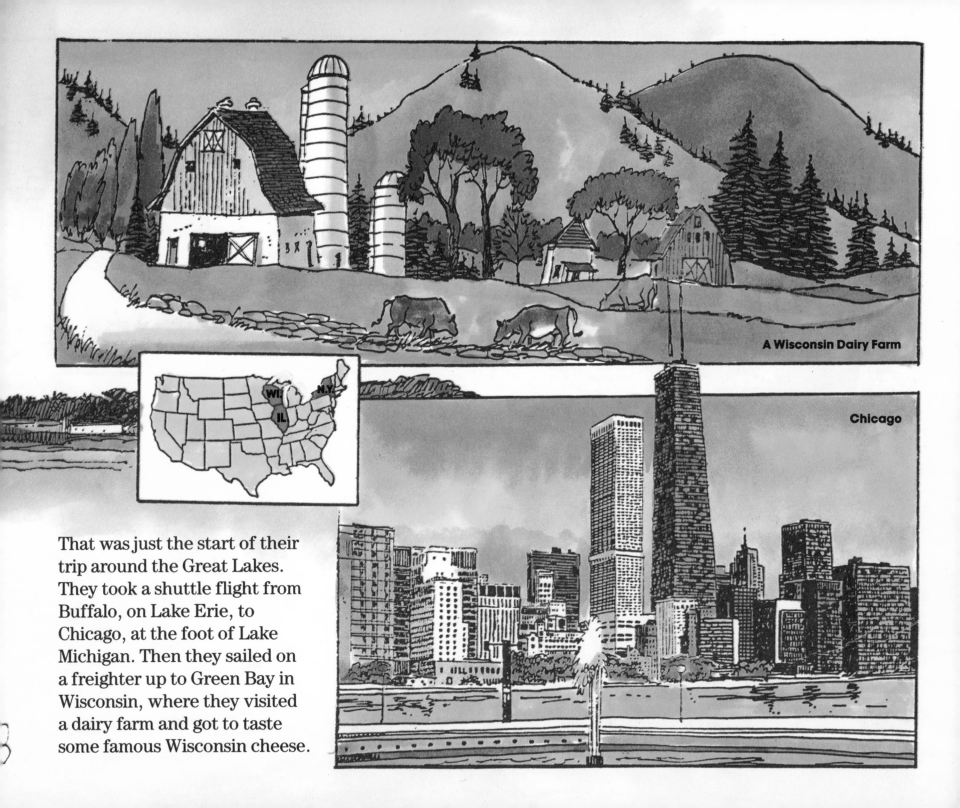

A Wisconsin Dairy Farm

Chicago

That was just the start of their trip around the Great Lakes. They took a shuttle flight from Buffalo, on Lake Erie, to Chicago, at the foot of Lake Michigan. Then they sailed on a freighter up to Green Bay in Wisconsin, where they visited a dairy farm and got to taste some famous Wisconsin cheese.

Frannie and Joey began their tour of the west at the Grand Canyon in Arizona. A mile below them, at the bottom of the red and yellow canyon walls, ran the rough white waters of the Colorado River.

"I'd like to go rafting down there," said Joey. "What an adventure!"

Hopi Indian Pueblos

In southern California they stopped to see the Palm Desert.

"These cactus plants are as big as trees," Joey exclaimed.

"Did you know," asked Frannie, "that all this was once the bottom of a great sea?"

The Palm Desert

Exploring the Hopi Indian pueblos in Gallup, New Mexico, was another adventure.

"They're sort of like an apartment building," said Frannie, "only they have ladders instead of elevators!"

CA. AZ. N.M.

"I know the names of all four presidents carved on Mount Rushmore," said Frannie. "There's George Washington, Thomas Jefferson, Theodore Roosevelt, and Abraham Lincoln."

Frannie and Joey were hiking in the Black Hills of South Dakota.

"Wild Bill Hickok lived near here, in Deadwood," said Joey. "This is real cowboy country."

When they traveled on to a dude ranch outside Denver, Colorado, they got to see a modern day cowboy riding a black bull.

They also visited the home of the Paiute Indians in Utah, where they saw tall pink, red and orange rocks with strange-looking faces on them. There are many legends about the rocks, including one about a hero named Coyote. He became angry when his people began to steal and fight, so he turned them into stone.

Coyote Rocks

Before leaving Utah, Frannie and Joey spent a night camping out in the Arches National Park. The next day they hiked over the great rock arches that rose out of the desert landscape.

"The west is full of such wonderful sights," Joey observed.

At Devils Tower in Wyoming, they saw a huge rock that stands 865 feet high. A Sioux Indian legend says that long ago, three Indian girls climbed the rock to escape from a bear. When the bear started to climb up after them the rock grew higher and higher, until the bear slid off, leaving its claw marks scratched into the side of the rock.

Old Faithful

Frannie and Joey went on to the Rocky Mountains, where they visited the Yellowstone National Park. They saw Old Faithful, the famous geyser that shoots clouds of hot water 150 feet up into the air every 65 minutes.

Frannie and Joey flew to San Francisco in northern California. Driving south on the Pacific Coast Highway in California, they stopped at the famous Lone Cypress on the Monterey Coast. As they gazed out at the peaceful waters of the Pacific Ocean, Joey suddenly shouted, "Look! Whales!"

Frannie saw them too. "They look so gentle," she said.

Every year, thousands of whales pass the California coast on their way north to their Arctic feeding grounds.

In San Francisco, they took a cable car down to the harbor.

They had a lunch of fresh crab at Fisherman's Wharf and took in the spectacular sight of the Golden Gate Bridge. This beautiful bridge was completed in 1937. Its main span measures 4200 feet—the third longest in the world.

San Francisco

The Golden Gate Bridge

CA.

"Timber!" yelled a lumberjack. Frannie and Joey were visiting a lumber camp on the western slopes of the Cascade Mountains in the state of Washington. They watched a helicopter bring a load of logs from the forest.

"In some camps," a logger explained, "they float all the logs down a river to the sawmill. But here we cart them down mostly by truck."

"Did you know that the paper used to make books comes from logs like these?" asked Frannie.

Mount Rainier

Frannie and Joey decided to fish for salmon in one of the region's many rich fishing streams.

"See that beautiful mountain in the distance?" asked Joey.

"Yes," replied Frannie. "That's Mount Rainier."

Alaska

There are several ways to get to the forty-ninth state, Alaska, including by ship from Seattle, Washington, or by airplane. Frannie and Joey chose to ride the Alaska Highway through western Canada.

"Did you know that Alaska is the largest state in the Union?" asked Joey.

On their way to the capital, Juneau, they stopped at Wrangell to see totem poles carved by Alaskan Indians. After visiting Juneau they went sledding into the interior where they saw Mount McKinley, the highest peak in North America.

Mount McKinley

King Kamehameha

Frannie and Joey boarded an airliner in Los Angeles that flew them across the Pacific Ocean to the fiftieth state, Hawaii. The plane landed in the capital, Honolulu, where they saw a beautiful bronze statue of King Kamehameha the Great, who was known as "The Napoleon of the Pacific." Through a series of wars, King Kamehameha unified the Hawaiian islands into a single kingdom.

Hawaii

"I feel like relaxing after our wonderful tour of the United States," said Frannie. This they did on the white sands of Waikiki, with Diamond Head mountain in view.

Your Passport Book

Follow these instructions to make your souvenir passport.

1. Carefully remove the next two pages from the book by tearing along the perforations on the left of each page.

2. Separate the pages into two by tearing along the perforations in the middle of each. Now you have four pieces that will form the pages of your passport.

3. Fold each of the four pieces in half along the line marked FOLD.

4. Beginning with the cover, place the folded pages in the correct order, like this:

5. Staple or sew the middle of the booklet to hold the pages together.

Now your passport is ready for use! There is space for the stickers you can find at the end of the book, and a place for your name and photo.

• Name a famous bridge in New York City.

Place stickers 1, 2, & 3 here.

• What is the statue that stands in New York Harbor?

Place stickers 4 & 5 here.

Frannie and **Joey**

PASSPORT BOOK

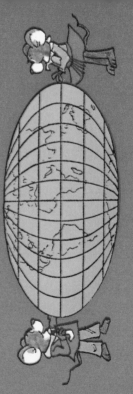

* Where was the Declaration of Independence signed?

Place stickers
11 & 12 here.

Place stickers
8 & 9 here.

* What is the famous historical relic in Philadelphia? *Hint: It has a crack in it.*

FOLD

Name

Date of Birth | Birthplace

Height | Hair color | Eye color

feet   inches

Place
your photo
here

Signature

FOLD

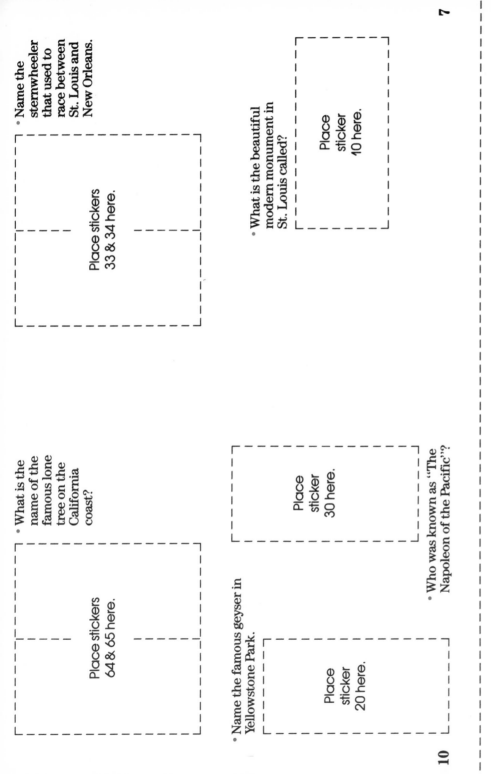

• Name the sternwheeler that used to race between St. Louis and New Orleans.

Place stickers 33 & 34 here.

• What is the beautiful modern monument in St. Louis called?

Place sticker 10 here.

• What is the name of the famous lone tree on the California coast?

Place stickers 64 & 65 here.

• Name the famous geyser in Yellowstone Park.

Place sticker 30 here.

Place sticker 20 here.

• Who was known as "The Napoleon of the Pacific"?

• Where does Congress meet?

Place stickers 13 & 14 here.

Place stickers 21 & 22 here.

• Where does the President live and work?

* Name the mountain in Georgia with carvings of three confederate generals.

Place stickers 25, 26, & 27 here.

* What is the name of the church in Boston associated with Paul Revere's ride?

Place sticker 17 here

FOLD

* Name a big city on Lake Michigan.

Place stickers 41 & 42 here.

Place stickers 45 & 46 here.

* Frannie and Joey visited a tremendous canyon in Arizona. What is it called?

FOLD

Use the rest of your Passport Book to arrange the remaining stickers.

* Which Indian tribe built unusual houses in New Mexico?

Place stickers 47 & 48 here.

* In South Dakota there is a famous monument to four presidents carved into a mountain. What is its name?

Place stickers 51, 52, & 53 here.

There are 70 stickers on this page and the following page. Follow the instructions in the passport booklet to find out where they belong.